Little Eco Experts

Ways to Repurpose, Reuse, and Upcycle

Translated by
Diana Osorio

How to be guardians of the planet

PowerKiDS press

Published in 2023 by PowerKids, an Imprint of Rosen Publishing
29 East 21st Street, New York, NY 10010

Cataloging-in-Publication Data
Names: Editorial Sol 90 (Firm).
Title: Ways to repurpose, reuse, and upcycle / by the editors at Sol90.
Description: New York : Powerkids Press, 2023. | Series: Little eco experts | Includes glossary and index.
Identifiers: ISBN 9781725337046 (pbk.) | ISBN 9781725337060 (library bound) | ISBN 9781725337053 (6pack) | ISBN 9781725337077 (ebook)
Subjects: LCSH: Recycling (Waste, etc.)--Juvenile literature. | Salvage (Waste, etc.)--Juvenile literature. | Waste minimization--Juvenile literature.
Classification: LCC TD794.5 W397 2023 | DDC 333.7--dc23

Coordination: Nuria Cicero
Editor: Alberto Hernández
Editor, Spanish: Diana Osorio
Layout: Àngels Rambla
Design Adaptation: Raúl Rodriguez, R studio T, NYC
Project Team: Vicente Ponce, Rosa Salvía, Paola Fornasaro
Scientific Advisory Services: Teresa Martínez Barchino

Imaging and infographics: www.infographics90.com
Firms: Getty/Thinkstock, AGE Fotostock, Cordon Press/Corbis, Shutterstock.

Manufactured in the United States of America

CPSIA Compliance Information: Batch #CSPK23. For Further Information contact Rosen Publishing, New York, New York at 1-800-237-9932.

CONTENTS

WHY GENERATE LESS GARBAGE?

Garbage Builds Up

There are materials that take thousands of years to decompose, which is why they build up and pollute the environment.

Built-Up Garbage

Garbage Incinerators

We generate a lot of garbage, and it increases every year. Garbage causes many problems in the environment because it contaminates the soil, water, and air, harming the planet and our health.

Burning It Can Pollute the Environment

It is often necessary to burn garbage in order to destroy it, which produces gases that cause global warming.

LESS CONSUMPTION, MORE RESOURCES

It is essential that we reduce the products we consume and the use of all natural resources. It is the best recipe to generate less waste.

Remember

In order to manufacture products of any type, raw materials are needed, which are those extracted from nature: water, energy, minerals, etc. These natural resources can be depleted and take time to renew. That is why we must take care of them and not overuse them!

THE GOAL

Let's try to reduce waste to less than 1.5 pounds (700 g) per person per day.

DID YOU KNOW?

Each type of material degrades at a different rate. Some do it quickly, whereas others take thousands of years.

Apple

From 1 day to 6 months

Wipes

3 months

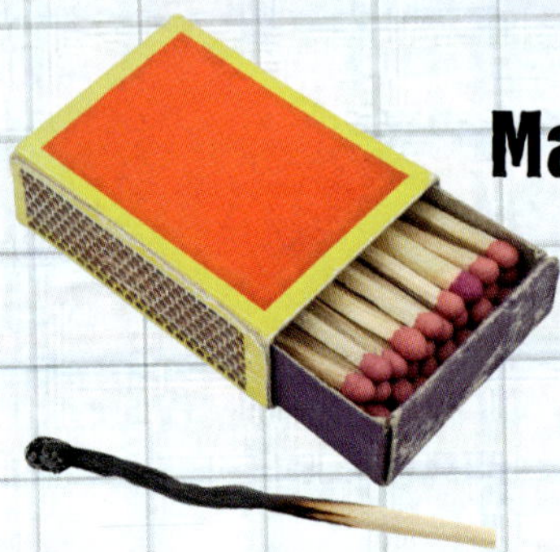

Matches

6 months

Candy

5 years

5 years

Bubble Gum

From 200 to 500 Years

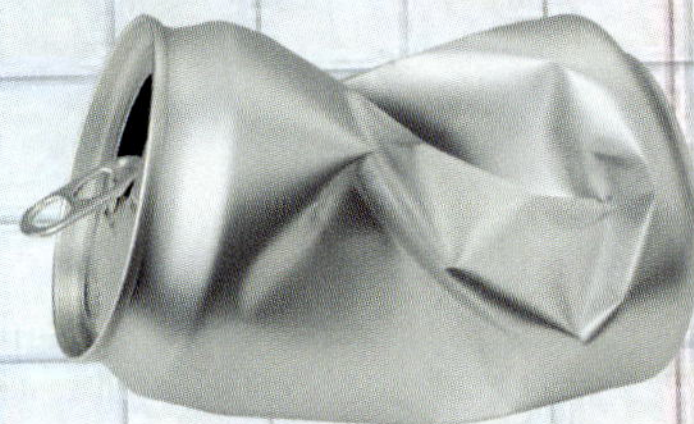

Can

Plastic Bag

From 200 to 1,000 Years

4,000 Years

Bottles

HOW TO REDUCE GARBAGE

Less Plastic Wrap

By not buying products that come wrapped in plastic, you will be reducing the use of products that pollute or are difficult to recycle.

Buy Only Necessary Things

Before buying something new, think if it really is necessary. Sometimes, without realizing, we buy things that we do not need.

Choose Reusable Bags

When you go shopping, take a basket, a cloth bag, or a cart, so you don't have to use plastic bags.

The key is to not generate unnecessary waste, to use products correctly, and to reuse or exchange.

Reuse Clothes

Think twice before throwing away clothes you no longer want. They can be used by your siblings or friends—or how about donating them to others with less resources?

Avoid Disposable Products

Limit the consumption of disposable products. Use cloth handkerchiefs instead of paper tissues.

WHAT CAN YOU DO?

You can be a superhero against garbage if you follow this super-easy advice:

1 Use Fewer Chemicals

Cleaning products can be toxic pollutants, and they come in plastic containers. If we reduce their use, we will pollute our rivers, seas, and oceans less.

Reuse!
Consume Responsibly!

2 Reduce the Use of Aluminum

Manufacturing aluminum requires a lot of energy and really creates pollution, so avoid using it as much as possible. How about replacing it with multipurpose containers?

3 Do Not Waste Paper

Reuse paper to write messages, practice math problems, or improve your handwriting. Take care of your pencils to make them last longer.

4 Print Responsibly

Use two-sided sheets of paper, and do not print what you can read on a computer screen.

REUSE IT!

Instead of using and throwing something out, we can extend the shelf life of products by reusing them. If we cannot reuse, we can use products that can be recycled.

Returnable Glass Containers

The best example of reuse is returnable glass containers, such as those for water, milk, or beer. In many countries, you pay extra for the container, but you get the money back when you return it.

If you reuse, you generate less garbage, and you will also save money.

Rechargeable Batteries

Batteries pollute. If we use rechargeable ones, we do the planet a favor.

HELP THE PLANET WITH IMAGINATION

Choose products with containers that can be reused or recycled, and before disposing of them, ask yourself if they are useful for anything. Most cartons can be repurposed—or reused for another purpose—to make crafts.

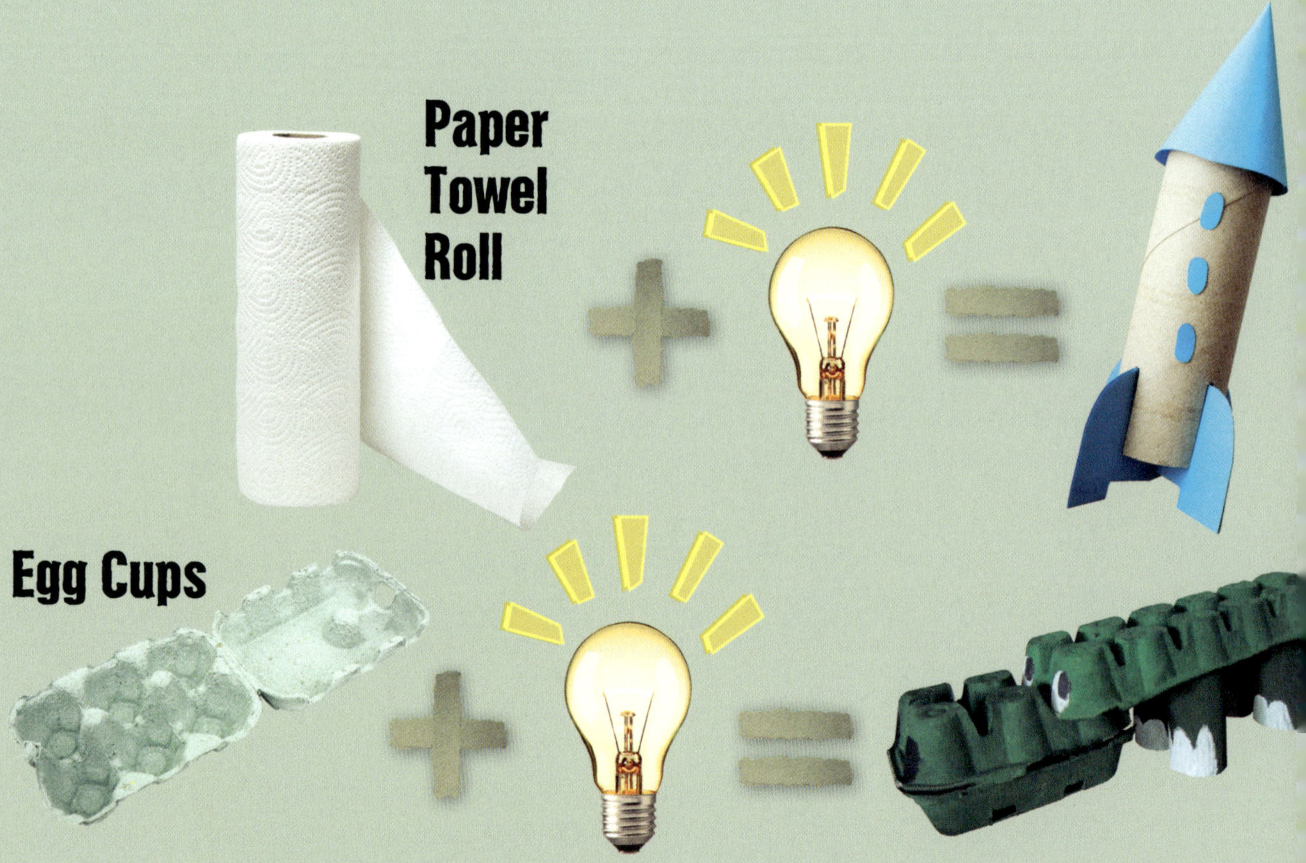

Underwater Example

With a plastic bottle, a balloon, a small straw, and a container filled with water, you can make a homemade submarine. By inflating and deflating the balloon inside the bottle, you will see how it floats or sinks.

Underwater Bottle

RESCUE THINGS FROM THE TRASH

Candleholder

Do you know how many things you can do with cans? Instead of throwing them away, you can turn them into a candleholder, a vase, or a tin-can telephone. Turning trash into something of value is called upcycling.

Vase

Tin-Can Phone

You can reuse old pots by turning them into planters.

Planter

Cardboard rolls can become practical pencil holders. Wrapped or painted boxes also have multiple uses.

Pencil Holder

Planter

Tire Swing

Even worn tires can be reused. If you have the overhead structure you need and some ropes, you can turn them into a swing.

HOW TO MAKE COMPOST

Instead of throwing it in the dumpster, we can use organic waste to make compost, a nutrient-rich fertilizer.

1 Look for a Container

This could be a wooden box or a flowerpot, for example. It is important that it is well ventilated.

2 Put the Waste Inside

First, make a base with leaves and twigs, and then make several layers of organic waste: fruit, eggshells, nuts, etc. Avoid meat and fish.

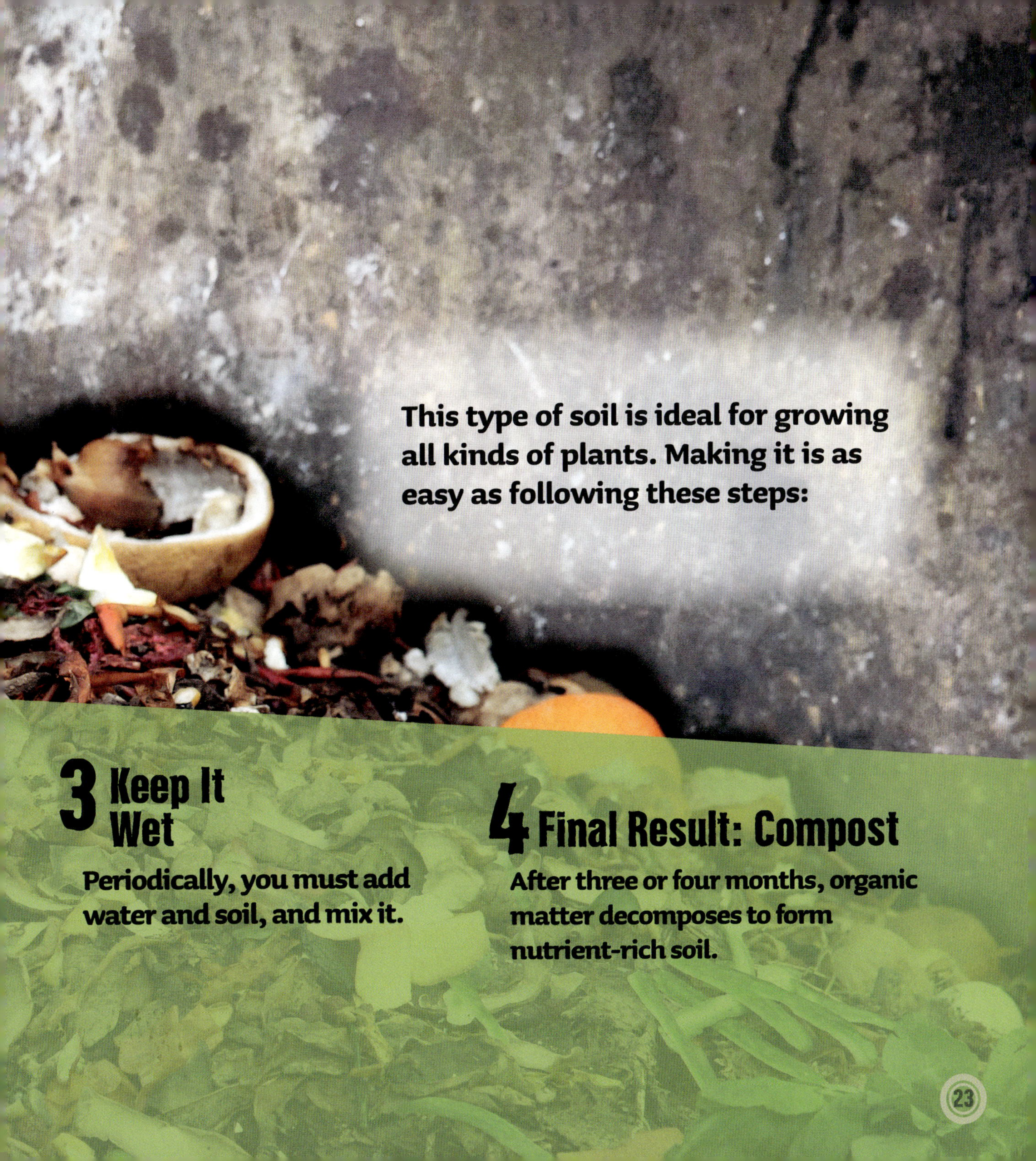

This type of soil is ideal for growing all kinds of plants. Making it is as easy as following these steps:

3 Keep It Wet

Periodically, you must add water and soil, and mix it.

4 Final Result: Compost

After three or four months, organic matter decomposes to form nutrient-rich soil.

HOW TO REUSE CLOTHES

When you outgrow clothes in good condition, they can be used by siblings, cousins, friends, or anyone who needs them.

Clothing Containers

Used clothes and shoes should not be disposed of with nonorganic garbage. There are special containers for this type of waste.

Charities

There are also charities that collect the clothes and deliver them to people with limited resources to buy new clothes.

Thrift Stores

Another option for clothes in good condition is to donate them to stores where they will be resold for charitable purposes.

DON'T THROW IT OUT!

If clothes are too old for reuse, you can always use them to make crafts, such as woven items using cloth strips or even rag dolls.

Old Clothes, New Rag

It is very common for some types of garments, such as T-shirts, to be reused as rags to clean the house, car, etc. Remember this, and reuse them.

Rag Dolls

CAUSE FOR CONCERN

Only one out of every five items of clothing manufactured ends up being recycled, whether to create new garments, rags, or carpets.

Only 20% of Clothes Are Recycled.

WHAT TO DO WITH OLD TOYS

Over time, some old toys stop being fun, but many are not broken. Before you throw them out, try to reuse them or think of other kids who might like them.

Charities

Mend for a Second Chance

AND BOOKS TOO

Never throw away books! You can exchange them with friends or donate them to a library or a charitable association.

Libraries

Street Markets

COASTAL CLEANING

Every year, tons of garbage is left on shores around the world. Waste contaminates beaches, and what is even worse, it reaches the seas and oceans. Ocean pollution is one of the most serious ecological problems in our world.

DID YOU KNOW?

Waste thrown into the sea causes thousands of animals to die each year. Some die trapped in ropes, nets, or plastics.

Every year, thousands of volunteers clean beaches and riverbanks. About 90 percent of the waste collected is related to recreational activities.

WHAT KIND OF GARBAGE IS USUALLY FOUND?

4%
Aluminum Cans

5%
Glass Bottles

8%
Plastic Bags

In the summer, many people visit the shores, especially the beaches. Those who are not aware of the need to take care of our planet, leave behind bags of food, plastic bags, cigarette butts, and other waste that usually end up in the ocean when the tide rises.

32%

Cigarette Butts

35%

Plastic Food-Packaging

16%

Other Waste

WHAT IS DECOMPOSITION?

Natural substances, such as food, decompose faster than artificial ones, such as plastic. Check this out!

YOU WILL NEED:

- Slice of bread
- Sheet of paper
- Plastic bag
- Paper and pencil
- Sticks
- Tape
- Garden shovel
- Watering can

STEP BY STEP: Find the instructions on the next page!

STEP ONE

Create three paper labels that say "BREAD," "SHEET OF PAPER," and "PLASTIC."

STEP TWO

With an adult's permission, dig three holes about 6 inches (15 cm) d
in the garden or in
a planter.

STEP THREE

Bury the bread, the paper, and the plastic bag in each of the holes. Place the labels, taped to sticks, at each hole.

STEP FOUR

Water the holes every three days. For the experiment to work, you must leave it buried for a month. When the month has passed, dig up the objects and see what happened.

Conclusion

The bread decomposed much faster because it does not contain chemicals like paper and plastic do.

Glossary

contaminate: to make something dirty, unsafe, or impure

decompose: to cause something to break down slowly

degrade: to cause something to break down into more basic parts

deplete: to reduce the amount of something by using it

fertilizer: matter added to soil to help plants grow

global warming: an increase in Earth's temperature thought to be caused by the increase of certain gases in the atmosphere, including carbon dioxide

nutrient: matter that living things need to live and grow

organic: having to do with living matter

ventilated: allowing air to enter

Index